COLLINS

Best Walks
ON THE
ISLE OF SKYE

by Richard Hallewell

HarperCollins*Publishers*

Published by Collins
An Imprint of HarperCollins*Publishers*
77-85 Fulham Palace Road
London W6 8JB

First published 1998

The walks in this guide were first published in
Bartholomew's *Walk Skye and Wester Ross.*

Printed in Italy

ISBN 0 00 4487087

98/1/16

CONTENTS

Symbols

WC   Public conveniences available at route, or in nearby town. (NB: these facilities are often closed in winter.)

👢   Hill walking equipment required. Strong boots; warm waterproof clothing; map and compass for hill routes.

🐾   Route suitable for dogs.

🚌   Public transport available to this route. Details given on individual routes.

Grade

A   Requires a high level of fitness and – for the hill routes – previous experience of hill walking. The use of a detailed map is advised.

B   Requires a reasonable level of fitness. Book map sufficient.

C   A simple, short walk on good paths.

Key map for the walks

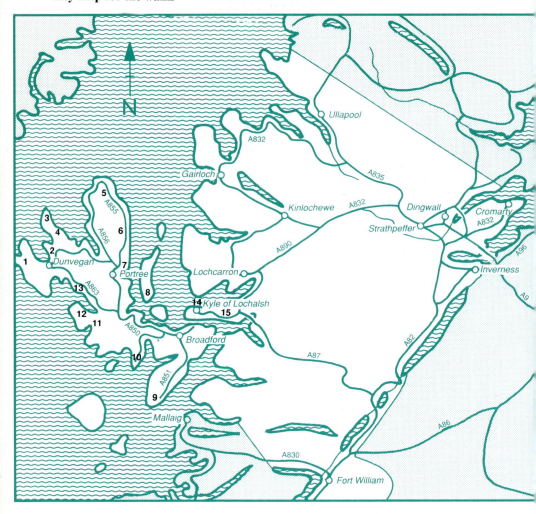

Key to map symbols

• • • •	Route
———	Metalled Road
+++++	Railway
Ⓟ	Parking
〰50m〰	Contour: shaded area is above height indicated

• • ❯ •	Direction of route
wc	Public convenience
🌲🌲	Coniferous woodland
♠♠	Broad-leaved woodland
i	Tourist information centre

1 foot = 0.3m
1 mile = 1.6km

INTRODUCTION

ABOUT THIS BOOK

This is a book of walks, each of which can be completed within one day. Each route is graded according to its level of difficulty, and wherever specialist hill walking equipment is required this is specified. There is a description of each route, including information on the character and condition of the paths, and with a brief description of the major points of interest along the way. In addition there is a sketch map of the route. Car parks, where available, are indicated on the route maps. The availability of public conveniences and public transport on particular routes is listed on the contents page, and at the head of each route. The suitability or otherwise of the route for dogs is also indicated on the contents page. The location of each route within the area is shown on the key map, and a brief description of how to reach the walk from the nearest town is provided at the start of each walk. National grid references are provided on the maps. The use of a detailed map, in addition to this book, is advised on all grade A walks.

Before setting out, all walkers are asked to read through the section of Advice to Walkers at the end of the Introduction. In the long term it never pays to become lax in taking safety precautions.

THE AREA

(Numbers in italics refer to individual walks.)
Like most of northern Scotland, the area is on the very edge of the area of comfortable human habitation: the population is small, and settlements are scattered thinly on the low land by the coast and along the occasional fertile glen.

When the last Ice Age retreated, some 8000 years ago, a landscape was revealed of steep-sided hills separated by wide valleys. The hills had been scraped down to the rock by the action of the glaciers: cracked and torn into dramatic peaks and narrow, broken ridges. The valleys were gouged into broad, U-shaped profiles, and were filled, in places, by saltwater inlets and freshwater lochs. The land was a poor, infertile one, but the landscape was, and remains, heroic in scale and form.

The Isle of Skye (apart from the Torridonian sandstone and gneiss of the southern part of the island) is composed of igneous rocks: basalt, granite and gabbro, formed when the molten magma from the interior of the Earth emerged onto the surface and cooled. These are hard rocks, which have produced, in places, some very dramatic effects: notably in the ridge of Trotternish (*5,6*) and the Cuillin Hills.

The island measures some 50 miles (80km) from Rubha Hunish in the north to the Point of Sleat (*9*) in the south, and around 25 miles (40km) at its widest point, between Neist Point (*1*) in the west and the eastern coast of Trotternish. The coastline is greatly indented, however, and the total land area is only around 670 square miles. The island is generally mountainous, but the peaks are low outside the tight group which constitutes the Cuillins: a tangled mass of rocky summits, ridges and corries, whose skyline is one of the finest sights in the Highlands. None of the routes in this guide enters the range (some experience of climbing is needed before venturing onto the steep slopes), but two of them (*10,11*) pass close by and provide fine views.

The main sea lochs around the island are Loch Snizort and Loch Dunvegan (*2*) in the north, and Lochs Bracadale (*13*), Scavaig (*10*) and Slapin in the west. The only large freshwater loch is Loch Coruisk, in the Cuillins, but there are numerous small rivers which are famous for their salmon and trout.

What little arable land there is is largely confined to the small-scale crofts along the coastal strip. The rest of the island is given over to rough sheep and cattle grazing, moorland and some forestry. The small population is scattered thinly around the coast of the island, sometimes collected into small crofting townships, but only forming towns at the island capital of Portree (*7*), and (to a lesser degree) at Dunvegan (*2*), Broadford and Kyleakin.

There are many smaller islands off the coast of Skye. The largest of these is Raasay (*8*), in the Inner Sound, which can only be reached by ferry from Skye. Amongst the many smaller, uninhabited islands is Oronsay (*13*) in Loch Bracadale, which can be reached on foot at low tide.

HISTORY

The earliest known inhabitants of the area were the Picts, whose various tribes occupied all of northern Scotland. They posed a serious threat to the northern boundaries of Roman occupation in Britain, yet their culture and language were subsequently to disappear almost entirely. They may have been of Celtic origin, but it is impossible to know for certain, and the only relics which they left were some items of metalwork, a collection of impressive stone carvings of uncertain purpose, and the advanced defensive structures known as brochs.

The carvings are thought to have been produced between the 6th and the 10th centuries. The earlier examples are decorated with abstract symbols and schematic animal forms, and may have represented family or tribal relationships; the later stones carry religious motifs.

The broch was a circular dry-stone tower, probably varying from 15 to 50 feet (4.6-15.2m) in height and with a single entrance. It was a defensive structure of the crudest form (presumably used as a refuge for surrounding tribesmen), yet the skill shown in the construction is often considerable.

The best examples in this area are Dun Telve and Dun Troddan, within a short distance of each other east of Glenelg (on the mainland), which are now retained in a well-preserved condition. Two less complete examples can be found near the path to Waternish Point on Skye (3).

From the 6th century onwards the Pictish communities throughout Scotland were increasingly on the defensive; harried in the south by the Britons and the Angles, and in the west by the Scots: a Celtic warrior-aristocracy which arrived from Ireland around 500 and established itself in the small kingdom of Dalriada in Argyll. The Scots were Gaelic-speaking and Christian, and their language and culture would gradually colonise virtually all of the area of modern Scotland.

In part, this was made possible by a further threat to all the tribes of Scotland: the increasing raids on the north and west, from around 800 onwards, by the Vikings. These coastal attacks affected both the Scots and the Picts, who seem to have moved inland under the pressure and may have been forced to work in concert to defend their territories. In 843 this trend was taken to its logical conclusion and the two kingdoms were unified under the Scot, Kenneth McAlpin.

The Vikings, meanwhile, established themselves in the northern and western islands, and (to a lesser extent) on the adjacent mainland. In succeeding generations they mingled with the existing populations of Picts and Scots to produce the mixed race of the Gallgaels. The resulting cultural mix varied from area to area: in the Northern and Western Isles the population largely adopted Norse language and customs, but elsewhere the earlier cultures survived in parallel (this seems to have occurred in Skye).

Nevertheless, the Hebrides remained under the overlordship of the Norwegian crown until after Alexander III had defeated King Haakon of Norway at the Battle of Largs (1263). Following this, Gaelic language and culture gradually ousted the Norse influence, until it had completely disappeared from the Highlands and western islands.

The net result of these various invasions was to create a society with strong warlike traditions and a disinclination to accept the nominal central control of the Scottish monarchy; a control which the monarchy – Norman and increasingly anglicised – could never fully enforce. As a result, a distinctive social organisation developed north of the Highland Line – tribal and semi-anarchic – which would survive until the greater powers of the Crown and Parliament of Great Britain could be turned against it in the 18th century.

The clan system emerged around the 13th century. It was based upon the unit of the family group – clann means children – and although it became flexible to the extent that individuals, or indeed whole clans, could ally themselves to a local power irrespective of any family relationship, the notion of kinship remained a part of the idea of the clan, and made the relationship between the chief and his clansmen different from the more strictly legal ties binding (for example) a feudal overlord and his vassal.

Warfare was part of the culture of the Highlanders, and although it would be inaccurate to suggest that the clansmen were perpetually at war with each other, it is true that feuding was endemic, and that individual inter-clan wars could be of very long duration. No single power ever evolved in the

Highlands which was sufficiently strong to enforce a lasting peace, so disputes could only be ended by either the complete victory of one of the antagonists or the intervention of neighbouring clans.

The nearest thing to a central government of Gaelic Scotland was the Lordship of the Isles: a hereditary title held by the MacDonalds. It was based upon the memory of Norse independence in the islands, but at its height extended to include much of the Gaelic-speaking mainland. A plot entered into by John of the Isles (whereby the Lordship would become an independent kingdom beneath the overlordship of the English king) led ultimately to the forfeiture of the title to the Scottish Crown in 1493. Thereafter, the Highlands lacked any single power strong enough to ensure internal stability.

There were a number of branches of the powerful Clan Donald within this area: the MacDonalds of Sleat (9), in the south of Skye (the Clan Donald museum is at Armadale), and also in the north of the island in Trotternish (5,6), from where they expelled the MacLeods; the MacDonells of Glengarry, with their main stronghold at Invergarry on Loch Oich; and the MacDonalds of Clanranald in the southwest. In addition to these, the main clans in the region were the MacLeods in the west of Skye, where Dunvegan remains the seat of the chief, (2) and in Raasay (8), and the Mackinnons in the east of the island.

Following the defeat of the Jacobites at Culloden, in 1746, clan society and the culture which it fostered began to disintegrate. The chiefs became landlords rather than the fathers of their tribe, and discovered a more pressing need for funds than for armed clansmen – particularly as these could no longer bear arms. Those who wished to continue the tradition of following a fighting life joined the newly formed Highland regiments and fought abroad for the Hanoverian monarchy; those who didn't left for the factories in the south or emigrated to the New World, either willingly or otherwise. In the Highlands, the inland glens were largely cleared for sheep farming, and the population was moved down to the coast.

PLACE NAMES

Most of the place names in the area covered by this guide are Gaelic: a language now known to comparatively few (though you will probably hear it spoken on Skye). A knowledge of the more common elements can add to the pleasure of walking in the area, and can also be of some help in map reading – a short list is included below. Even now, a certain amount of guesswork will be required, as the words which appear on the map will, as often as not, be slightly different from those shown here. In the more isolated areas of the west, where the language is still spoken, the names will be more grammatically correct, and will thus be altered by aspiration, the addition of letters to denote case, etc.

Gaelic is not the only language to have been spoken in this area, and place names can suggest the extent of the influence of the various peoples who have inhabited this part of Scotland through the centuries. Having said that, there are limitations to the effectiveness of this system: the Picts – who once inhabited all of this area; though not, presumably, in large numbers – have left virtually no indication of their presence in this form.

The Vikings were rather more influential, and a number of quite common Norse elements can be found; particularly in Skye and on the western seaboard. *Dale* for valley, *-ay* for an island (Raasay, Oronsay), *-val* for a hill (Stockval, Healabhal: both in Skye), *-nish* for a headland (Trotternish, Ullnish, etc). These can sometimes be found with added Gaelic elements (Healabhal Mhor), while occasionally the Norse word has simply been adopted by the Gaelic language (Sgeir from the Norse *Sker*).

Common elements in place names (Gaelic unless otherwise stated):

aber – confluence
abhainn – river
acarsaid – harbour
ach/Achadh – field
allt – burn
aird – promontory
-ay/-ey – island (Norse)
bal/baile – town, settlement
beag/beg – small
bealach – hill pass
beinn/ben – mountain
breac – speckled
buidhe – yellow
camas – bay
carn/cairn – hill, heap of stones
cnoc/knock – hillock

coire – corrie (hollow)
creag/cruig – rock, cliff
dale/dal – valley (Norse)
dubh – black
dun – steep hill, fort
eilean – island
firth – arm of the sea (Norse)
glas – Grey
inver – river mouth
kil – church
kyle/caol – narrow strait
leacann – slope
leitir – extensive slope
lochan – small loch
meall – rounded hill
mor – big
ruadh – red
rubha – point of land
sgeir/skerry – rock surrounded by sea
sgurr – peak, sharp top
sron – nose, point
stac – rocky column, cliff
storr – steep, high peak
tobar – well
-val – mountain (Norse)

NATURAL HISTORY

In order to describe the wildlife of the region, it is useful to provide a number of broad headings for the various habitats – **mountains and moorland, seashore, conifer woodland, broadleaved woodland** – and then to note the particular birds and animals which the walker may expect to see in each.

Mountains and moorland (*3,4,5,6,8,9,10,11, 12,14*). With the poor soils and heavy rainfall in the western part of the Highlands, moorland – generally confined to the higher slopes in the east – often remains the prevalent land cover right down to sealevel. Some **ptarmigan**, the hardiest of the grouse family, may be seen on the higher slopes, or lower in winter, but little else.

On the lower moors **red grouse** are present, with some **black grouse** (generally on the margins of woodland). The **wheatear** is common throughout the area during the summer, while the **stonechat** is present throughout the year. Of the waders, **snipe, curlew, golden plover, redshank** and **greenshank** are present, as are three types of falcon – **peregrine, kestrel** and **merlin** – plus the **buzzard, hen harrier, short-eared owl** and **golden eagle**. This latter is not uncommon amongst

the higher hills. **Crows** are also present: some **carrion crows**, but more generally the **hooded crow** and the **raven**.

The largest wild mammal in Britain is the **red deer**. These stay high in the hills during the summer – partly to escape the fierce insect life of the summer moors – but return to the lower moors during the winter. There are also local colonies of **sika deer** and **wild goats**. These last are not truly wild, but are the descendants of domestic animals, although individual herds may be of some antiquity. Carnivores include **wildcat, fox** and **stoat**, while the **mountain hare** – which, like the **ptarmigan** and **stoat** turns white in the winter – can also be found on the moors.

Seashore (*1,2,7,9,10,11,12,13,14*). The foreshore is generally of rocks (*1,7,9,13*) or cliffs (*1,11,12,13*) and one fine coral beach (*2*).

Rock type and boulder size have some effect on the life of the rocky foreshores, but the most important element is the degree of exposure to heavy seas. On exposed beaches the cover is limited to **lichens** and **barnacles**, while, in the sheltered lochs, there is a greater density of **seaweeds**, plus **mussels, limpets** and other shellfish. **Crabs** are common between the high and low water marks, while **sea urchins** and **starfish** can be seen just below the lowest tides. The shells of **scallops** and other bivalves are often thrown up along the beaches.

The **common seal** is the sea mammal most likely to be seen; lying on rocky islands and points. In addition, **otters** can sometimes be seen swimming in the sea; particularly in the evening.

Bird life includes a variety of gulls (**herring, common, black-headed, greater blackback** and **kittiwake**) and **terns** (common and arctic), plus **fulmar** and **gannet** around the cliffs, along with **razorbill, guillemot, puffin, cormorant** and **shag**. Waders include **curlew, oyster catcher, dunlin, redshank, sandpiper** and others, plus the **heron, mute** (on the southern part of the coast) and **whooper swans**, and **eider, teal, tufted duck, wigeon** and others.

In addition to these, the aerobatics of **ravens** are a feature of many cliff walks, particularly on Skye, while the **sea eagle** — quite recently reintroduced into Scotland on the island of Rum — might possibly be seen.

Conifer woodland (6,4,14,15). The commercial plantations provide cover for **rabbit, fox, wildcat, pine marten, roe deer** and others, but the trees are generally close together, thus keeping the sunlight from the forest floor and inhibiting the undergrowth necessary to sustain the smaller mammals and insects at the bottom of the food chain.

The bird life of the plantations can include **blue**, **great** and **coal tits**, **bullfinch** and **chaffinch**.

The Caledonian pine forest – a relic of the type of woodland which once covered much of the Highlands – is more open, and is comprised of Scots pine with a variety of broad-leaved trees and a rich undergrowth of heather and berries. The few remaining areas of this woodland are now protected, and are often fenced off to encourage regeneration.

Broad-leaved woodland (7,8,14,15). The type of trees generally encountered are **birch**, **rowan**, **hazel**, **holly** and **alder**, with patches of **oak** on south-facing slopes.

ADVICE TO WALKERS

Always check the weather forecast before setting off on the longer walks and prepare yourself for the walk accordingly. Remember that an excess of sunshine – causing sunburn or dehydration – can be just as debilitating as snow or rain, and carry adequate cover for your body in all conditions when on the hills.

Snow cover on higher slopes often remains well into the summer and should be avoided by inexperienced walkers as it often covers hidden watercourses and other pitfalls which are likely to cause injury. Also soft snow is extremely gruelling to cross and can sap energy quickly. Walking on snow-covered hills should not be attempted without an ice axe and crampons.

The other weather-associated danger on the hills is the mist, which can appear very swiftly and cut visibility to a few yards. A map and compass should always be carried while on the higher hills.

Obviously these problems are unlikely to arise on the shorter, simpler routes, but it is always wise when out walking to anticipate the worst and to be ready for it. The extra equipment may never be needed, but it is worth taking anyway, just in case. Spare food, a first aid kit, a whistle and a torch with a spare battery should be carried on all hill walks. In addition, details of your route and expected time of return should be left with someone, who you should advise on your safe return.

From August onwards there is grouse shooting and deer stalking on the moors. If you are undertaking one of the hill routes, first check with the local estate or tourist office, thereby avoiding a nuisance for the sportsmen and possible danger to yourself.

COUNTRY CODE

All walkers, when leaving public roads to pass through farmland, forestry or moorland, should respect the interests of those whose livelihood depends on the land. Carelessness can easily cause damage. You are therefore urged to follow the Country Code:

Guard against all risk of fire.

Keep all dogs under proper control (especially during the lambing season – April and May).

Fasten all gates.

Keep to the paths across farmland.

Avoid damaging fences, hedges and walls.

Leave no litter.

Safeguard water supplies.

Protect wildlife, wild plants and trees.

Go carefully on country roads.

Respect the life of the countryside.

1 Neist Point

Length: 1½ miles (2.5km) there and back
Height climbed: 300ft (90m)
Grade: C
Public conveniences: None
Public transport: None

A short lineal route, undulating steeply, leading out to a lighthouse on an exposed cape. Clear paths and wonderful views of surrounding sea cliffs.

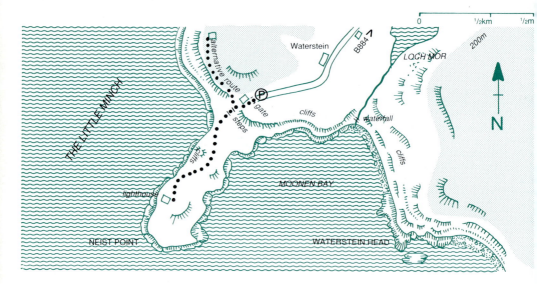

The Neist Point lighthouse is the most westerly on Skye, and it occupies a dramatic position on a narrow, grassy headland jutting out from a coastline of high cliffs. The short walk to the lighthouse is one of the pleasantest on the island.

To reach Neist Point, drive south from Dunvegan on the A863 for about a mile (1.5km), then turn right onto the B884. Follow this road (ignoring the numerous turns to right and left) for about nine miles (14.5km) until a road turns off to the left for Waterstein. Follow this for a little over two miles (3km) until the end of the road is reached. At this point there is a car park.

Go through the gate at the end of the car park and down the steep flight of steps beyond, leading down into the narrow neck of the headland. Looking to the left, there is a fine view of the tall cliffs of Waterstein Head, with a dramatic waterfall cascading down the lower cliffs beyond, while ahead are the cliffs on the northern side of Neist Point. This is a splendid place for birdwatching, with fulmars, gannets and ravens all likely to be seen.

From the low neck the path climbs again, leaving the highest part of the headland to the right then drops back down towards the lighthouse – 62f (19m), built in 1909 and now unmanned. Allow some time to explore the headland beyond the lighthouse, noting the fine views westwards to the Outer Isles, before returning by the same route.

From the car park there is an alternative, shorter route, out along the cliff-tops to the north. This walk provides a good view down to the lighthouse.

2 Coral Beaches

Length: 2 miles (3km)
Height climbed: Negligible
Grade: C
Public conveniences: None
Public transport: Bus service from Portree to Dunvegan Castle

A short lineal route through rough grazing land and by a rocky foreshore, leading to a fine shell and coral beach.

The Coral Beaches are unusual in being composed not of sand, but of a mixture of shell particles and tiny pieces of calcified seaweed. This produces a foreshore of a pale ochre colour, which turns to a fine turquoise when seen through the water at high tide.

To reach the beaches, drive to Dunvegan, then turn north along the A850 for a mile (1.5km) to the entrance to Dunvegan Castle: the seat of the Chiefs of the MacLeods. Traditions dating parts of the structure back to the 9th century are open to question, but there is no doubt that the MacLeods were in residence at least as early as the 14th century. This makes Dunvegan the oldest castle in Britain known to have been continuously inhabited by the same family. It is now open to the public and is well worth a visit while you are in the area.

Beyond the castle the road becomes single-track and continues for another four miles (6.5km) with Loch Dunvegan to the left. When the road reaches a T-junction at Claigan (near its conclusion), turn left, into a car park.

Walk through the gate at the far end of the car park (please note: no dogs allowed) and continue along the clear track beyond through an area of rough grazing. Pass through another gate (noting the sign warning about the bull) and continue along the track, which now runs behind the shore. After a short way a low ridge cuts across the route. Climb over this and continue along the rough footpath beyond to the Coral Beaches, backed by a pleasant area of cropped grassland.

From the end of the headland, beyond the beaches, there are fine views of the little islands of Isay, Mingay and Clett, near the mouth of the loch, and of the Waternish peninsula beyond.

Return by the same route.

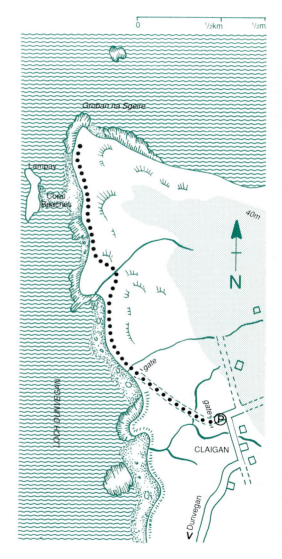

11

3 Waternish Point

Length: 8 miles (13km) there and back
Height climbed: Negligible
Grade: A
Public conveniences: None
Public transport: None

A clear lineal track through an area of rough grazing and moorland, leading to a ruined township. Fine views of coastal scenery.

This walk starts at the car park opposite the ruin of Trumpan Church, near the end of the Waternish peninsula. The church seems a peaceful spot now, but in 1578 it was the scene of a notorious atrocity, when a party of MacDonalds from Uist barred the door and set fire to the roof thatch with the congregation still inside. The raiders themselves were subsequently killed by a vengeful party of MacLeods.

To reach the church, drive three miles (5km) north of Dunvegan on the A850, then turn left onto the B886 road. Follow this until it turns down to the shore at Lusta, at which point a single-track road cuts right. Follow this for a further four miles (6.5km), ignoring the roads cutting off to the right, until the church is reached on a low hill overlooking the Minch.

From the car park, walk on along a straight section of road. When this turns right at a right angle, turn left, through a gate and on along a clear track (no dogs allowed, please note). Follow this track through a field, through another gate, then on across an area of rough grazing and moorland. The track is good and the route is never in doubt.

Apart from the tremendous views westwards, across the Minch to the Outer Isles, there are a number of points of interest along the way. The first is a monument, to the left of the track, commemorating Roderick MacLeod of Unish, who died hereabouts in battle with the MacDonalds of Trotternish in around 1530. A short distance beyond, to the right of the track, is the first of two brochs (Iron Age defensive structures) visible from the route. The second is a little under a mile (1.5km) further on. At the end of the track there are a number of ruins, including one of a substantial two storey house. Beyond these, an extra walk of two miles (3km) (there and back) leads to the lighthouse on Waternish Point.

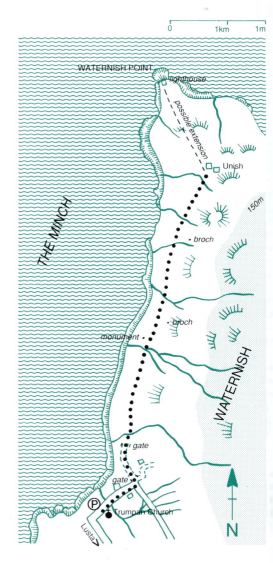

4 Waternish Loop

Length: 4-5 miles (6.5-8km)
Height climbed: 250ft (70m), undulating
Grade: B
Public conveniences: None
Public transport: Post bus service from Dunvegan to Gillen

A circuit on clear tracks and quiet public roads, through grazing land, moorland and conifer forestry. Fine views of coastal scenery.

To reach the Waternish peninsula, drive three miles (5km) north of Dunvegan on the A850, then turn left onto the B886. Follow this for four miles (6.5km) until it begins to turn down to the waterfront just beyond Lusta. At this point take the unnumbered road which cuts off to the right.

After a short distance the road enters a narrow band of woodland above Waternish House. One end of this route starts to the right of the road at this point, from a wide gateway beside a burn. If there is room, park by the side of this gateway; if it is not possible to do this without blocking the entrance then carry on until a convenient spot presents itself. If you are doing the whole circuit it is unimportant where you park, but if you are only doing the hill track, continue until the road for Gillen cuts off to the right. Follow this until it reaches a T-junction then turn right again. There is room to park at the end of the road.

Starting from the gate above Waternish House, walk up the clear track beyond, with grassland to either side. As the track climbs, the views to the south, of the islands and headlands around the mouth of Loch Dunvegan, begin to open up.

Continue along the track, by the left-hand edge of a stand of conifers (ignoring a track which cuts off to the right), then through the trees for a short distance before emerging on the far side of the hill. There are fine views ahead of Loch Snizort and the little Ascrib Islands, with the peninsula of Trotternish beyond.

A short distance beyond the trees the track splits. The right-hand track leads down to the shore of Loch Losait, while the left-hand track leads to the road end at Gillen. From this point either return by the same route or else follow the quiet public road back to the start.

13

5 Quiraing

Length: 4 miles (6.5km)
Height climbed: 950ft (290m)
Grade: A
Public conveniences: None
Public transport: None

A series of rough paths through an area of soaring cliffs and extraordinary rock formations. Tough going in places but extremely dramatic.

Quiraing (Norse for the 'Ridge of the Fold') provides one of the most dramatic areas of geological formations to be found in Skye – rivalled only by the Old Man of Storr *(20)*, about 11 miles (18km) south along the ridge of Trotternish. To reach it, drive some 19 miles (30km) north of Portree on the A855. From Brogaig, just north of Staffin, turn left on to the single-track road to Uig. Follow this for around two and a half miles (4km) and, just after the road has zig-zagged up the face of the ridge, park in the car park to the left of the road.

Start walking opposite the car park, and follow a rough but clear track which runs along the base of the cliffs, with a steep grassy slope dropping down to the right, and isolated rocky hills emerging from the grass on the far side of a rough valley. The most imposing of these is The Prison: a huge, tilted square block. Level with the northern end of this block, a shaft of rock about 120ft (40m) high, called The Needle, rises amongst the towering cliffs to the left of the path. (A rough scramble up the narrow gully to the left of this leads up to The Table: a patch of flat grassland high amongst the imposing buttresses of the cliffs. This detour adds to the distances shown above.)

Continue along the path beneath the foot of the cliffs: past a small lochan to the right and through a gap in a stone dyke, noting the knot of peaks and ridges visible ahead. When the ridge to the left reaches its lowest point, climb up on to it, then turn left again, back along the top of the cliffs (taking all due care). The initial climb up the slopes of Meall na Suiramach is gruelling, but the views (including a spectacular one down onto The Table from above) are magnificent.

After a little over a mile (1.5km) the car park becomes visible ahead.

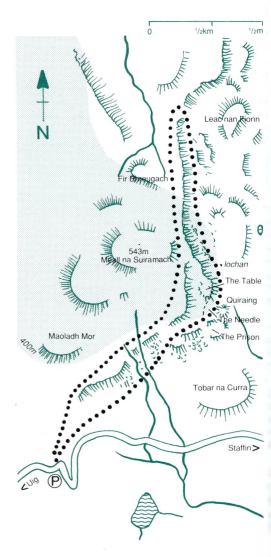

14

6 Old Man of Storr

Length: 3¹/₂ miles (5.5km)
Height climbed: 1000ft (300m)
Grade: B
Public conveniences: None
Public transport: Bus service between Portree and Staffin

A short, steep climb on rough tracks to an area of extraordinary and precipitous rock formations. Wonderful scenery; some care and sure-footedness required.

On an island rich in dramatic scenery, perhaps the most dramatic sight of all is the Old Man of Storr: a sheer pinnacle of rock, 160ft (49m) high, standing beneath the steep cliffs of The Storr (2360ft/719m). This famous geological curiosity is on the eastern side of the Trotternish peninsula, and can be reached by driving a little over six miles (9.5km) north from Portree on the A855 road for Staffin. Watch for the cliffs ahead and to the left, and park just before the start of a conifer plantation to the left of the road, near the northern end of Loch Leathan.

Cross a stile over the fence by the road, and walk up the slope beyond, with a dyke to the right and the plantation beyond that. The Old Man of Storr is visible ahead, with the buttresses of the Storr behind it, and a long line of cliffs sweeping away to the left. About half way up the edge of the plantation the path veers right, into the trees, and continues. It can be very wet under foot at this point.

Climb to the upper edge of the trees and look up the steep, grassy slope beyond. Beneath the massive cliffs there are two craggy protuberances like broken gateposts emerging from the grass. Start up the slope and aim to pass between them. The path is a steep one, but it is worth the effort, for once through the gap the route enters an area of extraordinary geological contortions. There are a number of paths beyond. Follow (carefully) whichever you prefer, through the cliffs and boulders, until the base of the Old Man is reached.

From this point there are splendid views across the Sound of Raasay, and south to the hills of southern Skye. The plantation is visible below, with a clear path running down to its left-hand edge. Follow this down to the road, then turn right to return to the start.

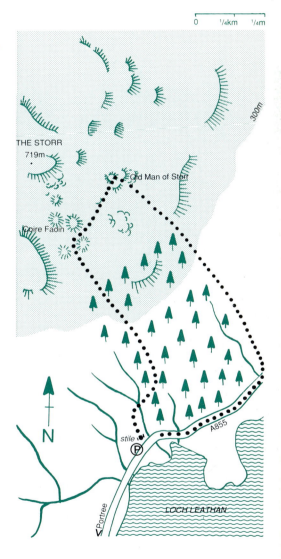

15

7 Portree Loop

Length: 2¹/₂ miles (4km)
Height climbed: 400ft (120m)
Grade: B
Public conveniences: Portree
Public transport: Numerous bus services to
Portree

A short loop on rough paths (which can be damp in places) through grazing land and woodland and along a rocky foreshore. Fine coastal scenery.

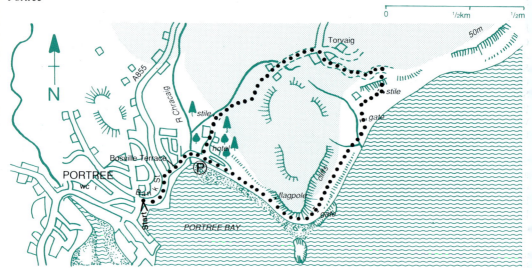

Portree is the administrative centre for Skye: a small, tight knit town clustered about a sheltered bay. The name means 'King's Harbour' – a reference to a visit paid to the island by King James V in 1540 – although the town itself was not developed until the 19th century.

This route leads out around the headland to the north of the bay, and starts from the town centre. Walk north up Bank Street, then turn right along the curving Bosville Terrace, from where there are fine views down into the busy anchorage. Keep right at the next two junctions, swinging east along the northern shore of the bay. Just after passing a parking area to the right, there is a split: the road heading off ahead left, the path (signposted 'jetty') continuing by the bay.

The path is quite clear at this point, and remains so as far as the viewpoint and flagpole (commemorating the association of the Nicolson

clan with the area), but becomes rougher beyond, as it swings round the steep headland.

Just beyond the point there is a gate in a dyke. Go through this and continue across damp grassland, with a fence to the right, until another fence crosses the way. Turn left along this until a gate is reached; go through this and continue around the edge of the field beyond. At the top of the field there is a stile. Cross this and climb up the slope beyond before turning left along a clear track, climbing to the top of the hill.

When the track reaches the houses at Torvaig, take the track beyond the house to the left, heading down towards two large farm buildings. Pass between these and then continue across rough moorland, with Portree visible in the valley ahead.

Cross a stile as the path enters an area of woodland, then continue downhill, passing to the right of a hotel, before rejoining the original road near the car park.

8 Hallaig

Length: 5 miles (8 km)
Height climbed: Up to 800ft (250m), undulating
Grade: A/B
Public conveniences: None
Public transport: Ferry service to Raasay from Skye

A fine route on tracks and footpaths of varying quality, passing through areas of woodland, grazing land and moorland, and leading to a deserted township. Excellent views.

Raasay is a narrow island, running some 15 miles (24km) north to south and lying between Skye and Applecross on the mainland. It is reached from Skye by a ferry running from Sconser – three miles (5km) east of Sligachan – to the pier at East Suisnish. Please note that the distances shown for this route assume the use of a car (though a bicycle would provide more pleasure on these quiet roads) for the four miles (6.5km) to the start of the route.

Turn left from the pier as far as Inverarish, where a road cuts off to the right. Follow this, and at the next junction turn right again and follow the road across the moor to its conclusion at North Fearns. There is space for parking just before the last house on the road, beyond which a clear track continues.

Follow the track along the face of a wooded slope, with fine views across to Applecross and the islands of the Inner Sound. The track soon emerges from the wood and then continues, with the cliffs of Beinn na Leac up to the left, to a turning point above the little headland of Rubha na Leac. At this point there is a memorial cairn to 'the people of Hallaig and other crofting townships' (who were cleared from the land during the last century), and a splendid view opens up of the steep, straight slopes of the eastern coast of the island. Also, in the nearer foreground, there is a fine waterfall where the Hallaig Burn drops over a low cliff into the sea.

Beyond the headland the path gradually deteriorates and finally disappears by the Hallaig Burn. Cross the burn and climb up the slope beyond to visit the deserted township. From this point, either return by the same route or follow the burn up to its watershed and there join the rough path by the side of Beinn na Leac. This path eventually disappears, but not before the public road appears below. Turn left along this to return to the start; right to return to the pier.

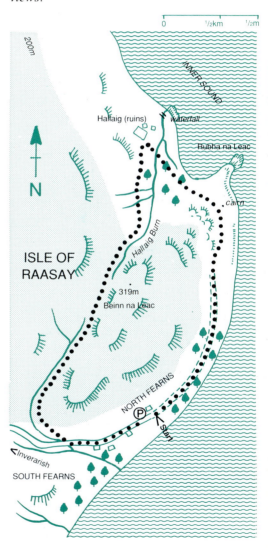

17

9 Point of Sleat

Length: 4-5½ miles (6.5-9km)
Height climbed: Undulating
Grade: B
Public conveniences: None
Public transport: None

A clear, lineal track through hummocky moorland leading to a tiny, rocky harbour, and to the lighthouse beyond. Fine moorland and coastal scenery.

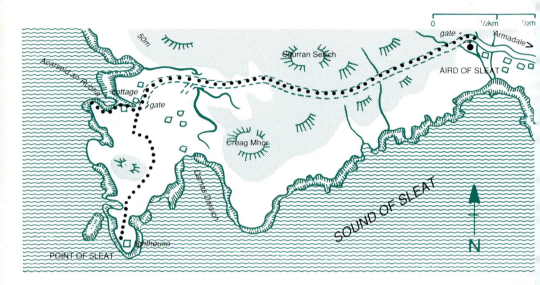

The peninsula of Sleat forms the most southerly part of the island of Skye, with the narrow Sound of Sleat separating it from Knoydart on the mainland to the east. Its scenery is somewhat gentler than that found in most of the island. It boasts, in addition, the pleasant little harbour of Isle Oronsay, and the Museum of the Isles at the Clan Donald Centre, Armadale House (once home to Lord MacDonald: descendant of the old line of MacDonald Lords of the Isles); well worth a visit while you are in the area.

This pleasant lineal walk leads down towards the Point of Sleat. To reach the start, drive south from Broadford on the A851 to Armadale. When the road swings left, down to the ferry pier, carry straight on for about five miles (8km), following the winding single-track road to its conclusion at the small church at Aird of Sleat. Parking is very limited here, and it may be necessary to drive a

short distance back along the road to find somewhere suitable (ie, where you are not blocking the roadside gates and passing places).

Go through the gate at the end of the road and follow the clear track beyond as it meanders through an area of heather moorland, with views over the surrounding sea opening up from the higher sections of the track. Shortly after crossing a bridge over a burn, the track splits. Keep to the right and continue, down to a gate by a cottage. Immediately beyond this, a rough track cuts left, leading a little over half a mile (1km) to the lighthouse on the point.

Alternatively, carry straight on after the gate, down to the tiny natural harbour. A short scramble over the rocks beyond, out to the point to the left of the harbour, provides a fine view southwards to the islands of Eigg and Rum.

Return by the same route.

10 Elgol

Length: Up to 9 miles (14.5km)
Height climbed: Undulating; 650ft (200m) on long return route
Grade: A/B
Public conveniences: Elgol
Public transport: Post bus service from Broadford

A long circuit on rough footpaths and quiet public roads. Some care needed in places, but matchless views of the dramatic Cuillin Hills on clear days.

To reach the start of this route, drive 14 miles (23km) south of Broadford on the winding B8083, which ends at the little settlement of Elgol on the slopes above Loch Scavaig, near the end of the Strathaird peninsula. As the road drops down towards the shore, look for the car park on the right-hand side.

To start the route, walk back up the road for a short distance, then turn left along a track (initially tarmac) behind some houses, signposted for 'Gàrsbheinn'. By the last of the houses there is a sign for a footpath to Coruisk. Follow this.

The rough path starts along a steep, grassy slope, with wonderful views (even from the earliest sections of the route) across Loch Scavaig to the island of Soay and the craggy peaks of the Cuillins. Beneath Ben Cleat the slope becomes even steeper, and sufferers from vertigo may not wish to follow the path any further. For the rest, continue across the foot of Glen Scaladal (crossing the burn can prove difficult when it is in spate, but it can usually be achieved dryshod), then on along the path beyond beneath Beinn Leacach to the bay at Camasunary, with its grassy hinterland overshadowed by the huge buttresses of Sgurr na Stri and Blà Bheinn.

From this point, the shortest return is by the same route. Alternatively, look for the clear track which winds up the right-hand side of Abhainn nan Leac and over the hills to the east. The track runs for a little under three miles (5km) before joining the B8083, climbing to around 650ft (200m) at its highest point. Turn right along the road (generally quiet) for about three and a half miles (5.5km) to return to Elgol.

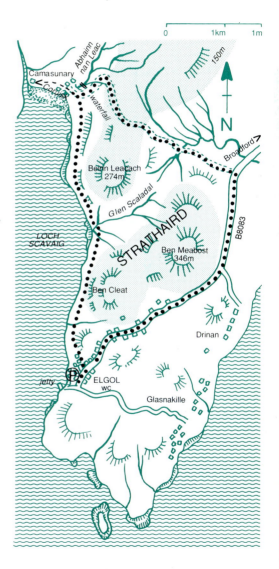

11 Glenbrittle

Length: 6 miles (9.5km) there and back
Height climbed: Undulating
Grade: A
Public conveniences: Camp site
Public transport: None

A long, lineal route on rough paths across rugged grazing land. Some navigation required when paths peter out at far end of route. Fine coastal scenery.

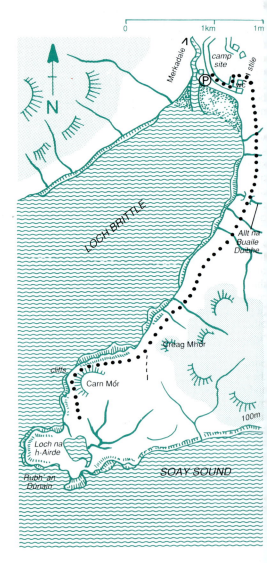

Glen Brittle curves around the western edge of the Cuillin Hills, and the car park at the point where the river empties into Loch Brittle is a favoured starting point for many of the routes through this dramatic range. These routes require some climbing experience, however, and none are described in this guide (those who are interested in the hill routes can obtain details locally). It is not necessary to take to the hills in order to find good walking, however, and there is a very pleasant coastal route running southwards from the car park towards the headland of Rubh' an Dùnain.

To reach the start of the route, drive west from Sligachan on the A863. After six miles (9.5km) the B8009 cuts off to the left. Follow this for about two miles (3km) to Merkadale, then turn left again on the unnumbered road for Glenbrittle. After about eight miles (13km) the road reaches the camp site at the head of Loch Brittle. Park in the spaces by the road and walk on into the camp site. Look for the public conveniences to the right of the road and walk down to the left of them, then cross the stile over the fence beyond. Two paths head off to the right – they run parallel, so either will do.

Continue along the slope above the loch. The ground can be very wet, and some agility may be required to cross the various burns which flow down the slope towards Loch Brittle, but the largest of these (Allt na Buaile Duibhe) does have a bridge across it.

After two and a half miles (4km) the path climbs up and around the shoulder of Creag Mhór. From this point there are views of the islands of Rum and Canna, while the rough path can be seen to split in the low ground beyond the hill. Either path will lead on down to Loch na h-Airde, but the right-hand route, along the cliff edge beneath Carn Mór, is drier, clearer and more dramatic.

12 Talisker

Length: 5^1/$_2$ miles (9km)
Height climbed: 400ft (120m), undulating
Grade: B
Public conveniences: None
Public transport: Bus service between Portree and Fiskavaig

A pleasant route on clear tracks; through rough grazing land at first and leading to a wide bay flanked by sea cliffs.

To reach the start of this route, drive five miles (8km) west of Sligachan on the A863, then turn left on the B8009. From Portnalong, turn left onto the road signposted for Fiskavaig. Some three miles (5km) along this road there is a severe hairpin bend. Look for a space to park here (being careful not to block any gateways).

Go through the gate by the hairpin and start walking along the track beyond; leading southwards through the rough grazing land of a shallow valley, with peat cuttings down to the left of the track. As the track continues, the rocky mass of Preshal More – looking a little like the half-eroded Sphinx in the Valley of the Kings – becomes clearer on the far side of Gleann Oraid.

After a little over a mile (1.5km) the track zig-zags down into the valley beside a waterfall. At the foot of the slope there is a cottage. Pass to the right of this and continue along the clear track beyond; through a farm and on to a metalled road. Two roads cut off to the right. Ignore the right-hand one (a private entrance to Talisker House) and take the other; with a steep slope to the left and a wall to the right with deciduous woodland beyond.

The track passes Talisker House and crosses a burn, immediately beyond which there is a sign to the right, indicating the 'scenic walk to the sea', and a gate. Go through this and follow a clear path by the side of the burn, flanked by trees and meadows full of wild flowers, down to the stony beach at the head of Talisker Bay. From here there are fine views of the great sea-cliffs to the north and south. Note the splendid waterfall cascading down the cliffs to the north of the bay.

Turn left along the shore to join a clear track which leads back up to Talisker House, then return by the original route.

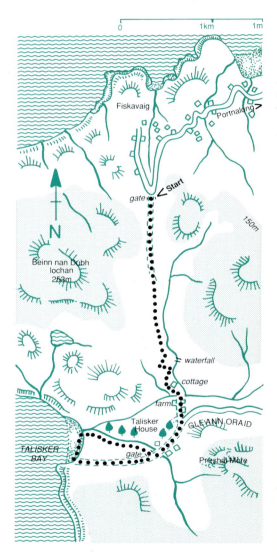

21

13 Oronsay

Length: 3 miles (5km) there and back
Height climbed: Up to 250ft (70m), undulating
Grade: C
Public conveniences: None
Public transport: None

A short, lineal route through rough grazing land to a small, grassy island (cut off at high tide). Paths can be wet, but fine sea cliffs and coastal scenery.

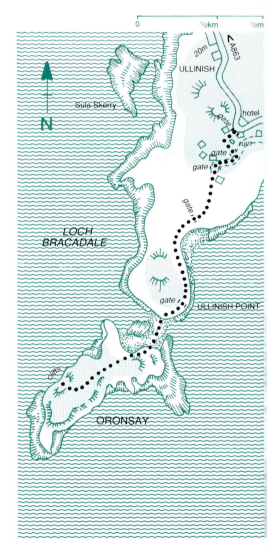

The name 'Oronsay' – quite common in the Scottish islands – is of Norse origin, and means 'tidal island'. This particular Oronsay remaining true to its name, **it is important to check the state of the tide before crossing.** The tidal section of the route is only short, and the island itself small enough to be crossed in a few minutes, but there is no point in risking becoming cut off.

To reach the route, drive nine miles (15km) south of Dunvegan on the A863, then turn right on the single-track road signposted for Ullinish. After a little under two miles (3km), park near the hotel. Go through a gate between the buildings opposite the hotel and follow the path beyond until the remains of a building appear to the left. Turn left, across an open area, to a small gate leading on to a metalled road. Turn right and follow this until a gate is reached to the right of the road, just before the last house.

Go through the gate and continue along a clear track. When a bay comes in from the left there is a second gate, beyond which the path becomes narrower, and can be very damp, but remains clear. Follow this to a further gate, near the end of the headland, beyond which the rough path drops down through a gully to the causeway of loose stones leading across to the island.

There are no buildings on the island, but the cropped grass provides pleasant walking, and there are dramatic cliffs around the western end. To get the best views around Loch Bracadale, climb up to the highest point (being careful when approaching the summit as the cliffs drop sheer immediately beyond). To the west is Wiay, and the smaller Harlosh and Tarner Islands, with Idrigill Point and Macleod's Maidens beyond. To the east is the lighthouse on Ardtreck Point, at the mouth of Loch Harport, while to the south the cottages of Fiskavaig are visible above the low cliffs *(12).*

14 Plockton Loop

Length: Up to 7 miles (11km)
Height climbed: 600ft (180m)
Grade: B/C
Public conveniences: Plockton
Public transport: Post bus service from Kyle of Lochalsh

A possible circuit, starting on a clear footpath by the shore and continuing through a variety of types of woodland and farmland. Clear tracks and quiet public roads.

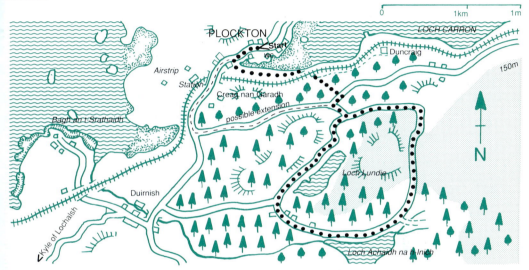

The little village of Plockton is just over five miles (8km) north of Kyle of Lochalsh along minor roads. It is one of the pleasantest settlements on the coast: a couple of streets of small houses and hotels spread along the edge of a shallow, well-protected anchorage. Looking north from the bay there is a fine view of the islands and rocky, wooded headlands around the mouth of Loch Carron, with the dramatic mountain scenery of Wester Ross visible beyond.

For this route, walk south from the centre of the village. When the bay ends to the left, there is a signpost for a footpath to Duncraig. Turn left onto this and follow it around the head of the bay, and then on between the railway line and the shore. There are fine views of the village and its anchorage from this stretch of path.

After a short way the path ducks under the

railway line and starts to climb the wooded hill behind. A path cuts off to the left (to Duncraig); ignore this and carry on, climbing gently through the trees to join a quiet public road.

Turn right along the road to reach a junction. For a short route, turn right and follow the public road two and a half miles (4km) back to Plockton. For a longer walk, turn left, then left again at the next junction, and follow a narrow road through mixed woodland in a loop of a little under four miles (6.5km). Keep to the right at each junction, passing Loch Achaidh na h-Inich and Loch Lundie along the way; pleasantly situated amongst tree-covered hills. Be careful to shut the forestry gates behind you.

When the loop is complete, return either by the original path or by the alternative route along the public road previously mentioned.

23

15 Balmacara Forest Walk

Length: 2-4 miles (3-6.5km)
Height climbed: 400ft (120m)
Grade: B
Public conveniences: None
Public transport: None

Two fine forest walks on clear, signposted paths; passing through both conifer and broad-leaved woodland, and providing excellent views (particularly from the longer route).

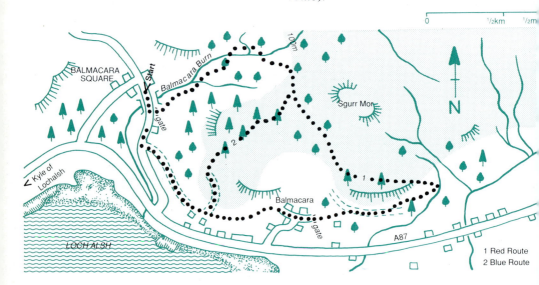

These two routes start from the little village of Balmacara Square, in a valley to the north of Loch Alsh. To reach it, drive three miles (5km) east of Kyle of Lochalsh on the A87, then turn left onto a minor road.

Park in the village then walk south on the eastern exit road. After a short distance the road crosses the Balmacara Burn, and just beyond this there is a gate to the left signposted for the 'forest walk'. Follow this path along the burn side, with the slopes of Sgurr Mor visible ahead, until it enters the conifer plantation and begins a steep ascent. Once the climb has levelled out the path crosses the burn, then recrosses it, before climbing up to join a clear track. Turn right along this.

After a short distance a smaller path cuts off from the main track (just before it enters an area of beech woodland). For the shorter (blue) route,

continue down the main track; for the longer (red) route take the higher path, leading on along the slope of the hill, the trees gradually clearing to allow wonderful views of Loch Alsh, the narrow sound of Kyle Rhea and the surrounding hills of Skye and the mainland.

The path continues round the hill until it reaches a burn flowing down the slope through an area of oakwood, at which point it drops down to join a clear track. Turn right and at the first junction keep to the left (there is a post indicating the route). Shortly after this a gate is reached, beyond which a road continues in front of a house.

Continue to the next house, then join a rougher path which continues through an area of gorse. At the next junction (at which the shorter route rejoins) carry straight on, back to the public road. Turn right to return to Balmacara Square.